The Way to Vict'ry

The Way to Vict'ry

Haiku

ILLUSTRATED BY
Cristina Basile

Stephen Wendell

Peregrine Publishing
Paris

Peregrine Publishing
www.stephenwendell.com

Copyright © 2017 Stephen Wendell

Illustrations © 2017 Cristina Basile

Original edition text © 2016 Stephen Wendell

All rights reserved. Published 2017.

Original edition published 2016.

First Edition

Paperback

Illustrations courtesy of Cristina Basile.

Cover illustration:

The way to vict'ry

by Cristina Basile.

Courtesy of the illustrator.

ISBN 979-10-96666-21-8

À tous les gentils connus cette année

–Cristina Basile

For Peregrine

–Stephen Wendell

Contents

Preface to the Illustrated Edition   vii

Preface to the Original Edition   ix

The way to vict'ry   3

Let go the ego   5

Leap from a high branch   7

Preface to the Illustrated Edition

> I want to create beautiful images, suggestive, evocative, and not all together realistic, where the color lends value to certain passages, and the perspective gives way to leave space for the poetry.

The illustrator wrote those words, here translated from French, following our serendipitous meeting at a book fair. Mentioning a project to produce an illustrated book of haiku, I had explained the idea to give the artist carte blanche to interpret each poem while expressing her own style.

After a fruitful collaboration between artist and poet, I am pleased to present the work of Cristina Basile in this illustrated edition of *The Way to Vict'ry*.

S. W.

Preface to the Original Edition

In Sun Tzu's *Art of War*, the fifth-century BC Taoist author likens the successful battle plan to a watercourse: it follows the path of least resistance to its objective.

Buddhist monk Matthieu Ricard devotes a chapter of his book *Happiness* (Atlantic Books, 2012) to the ego. He suggests the ego, imposed as a shield, becomes a target, which attracts suffering.

These works inspired the first two haiku in this book.

And the magpie flight instructor? It's one of a mated pair that makes its nest in the bay tree behind the house. The springtime garden is a cacophony of young magpies on flight training day.

In haiku form, the lessons are easier to retain. These three have become personal mantras.

Stephen Wendell
November 9, 2016
Paris, France

The Way to Vict'ry

The way to vict'ry

Flows, like the river, downhill–

In life as in war

Let go the ego

Ever so fragile a thing;

Let the spirit soar

"Leap from a high branch;
Spread your wings to catch yourself."

–Magpie teaching flight

About the Illustrator

As a teenager, **Cristina Basile** drew ballerinas on a studio bench during dance class to memorize the moves. Thus was born a passion to interpret movement as visual art.

Cristina earned an undergraduate degree in Illustration from the International School of Comics in her native Rome and a Master's in Motion Design from the Gobelins School of Visual Communication in her beloved Paris, which is home since 2012. This is her third illustrated book.

If you enjoyed this book, please tell your friends about it and consider leaving a short review on your preferred retailer site with as many stars as you think it worthy:
smarturl.it/basilevictry

To see more of Cristina's work,
visit her online portfolios:

www.behance.net/cristinabasile

www.artfinder.com/cristina-basile

About the Author

Stephen Wendell studied philosophy at East Tennessee State University in the 1980s. Since then his way has been mostly downhill.

If you enjoyed this book, please tell your friends about it and consider leaving a short review on your preferred retailer site with as many stars as you think it worthy:
smarturl.it/basilevictry

FOLLOW STEPHEN'S NEXT ADVENTURE ON
A Peregrine's Path
EXPLORATION—DISCOVERY—ADVENTURE

www.stephenwendell.com/aperegrinespath

Other books by the same author

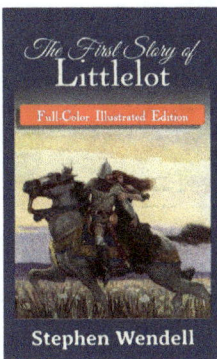  

In e-book and paperback editions from

Peregrine Publishing
www.stephenwendell.com/books

www.ingramcontent.com/pod-product-compliance
Lightning Source LLC
LaVergne TN
LVHW020420070526
838199LV00055B/3677